D0948138

Places We Go

A KIDS' GUIDE TO COMMUNITY BUILDINGS

by Rachelle Kreisman
with illustrations by Tim Haggerty

RED
CHAIR
·PRESS·

Please visit our website at **www.redchairpress.com** for more high-quality products for young readers.

Publisher's Cataloging-In-Publication Data
(Prepared by The Donohue Group, Inc.)

Kreisman, Rachelle.
    Places we go : a kids' guide to community buildings / by Rachelle Kreisman ; with illustrations by Tim Haggerty. -- [First edition].

    pages : illustrations ; cm. -- (Start smart: community)

    Summary: Learn about the buildings in both large and small communities that provide goods or services and make these communities more livable. Includes fun facts.
    Interest age level: 006-009.
    Edition statement supplied by publisher.
    Includes index.
    Issued also as an ebook.
    ISBN: 978-1-939656-91-9 (library hardcover)
    ISBN: 978-1-939656-92-6 (paperback)

    1. Community life--Juvenile literature. 2. Libraries--Juvenile literature. 3. Schools--Juvenile literature. 4. Postal service--Juvenile literature. 5. Hospitals--Juvenile literature. 6. Community life. 7. Libraries. 8. Schools. 9. Postal service. 10. Hospitals. I. Haggerty, Tim. II. Title.

HM761 .K742 2015
307   2014957485

Illustration credits: p. 1, 7, 13, 15, 17, 19, 20, 21, 23, 25, 26, 28, 32: Tim Haggerty

Photo credits: Cover, p. 1, 9, 10, 12, 14, 16, 22 (inset), 27 (bottom): Marisa Burntitus for RCP; p. 5, 15, 18 (inset): iStock; p. 4, 6, 8 ,11 (left), 13, 17, 20, 21, 22 (large), 23, 24 (inset), 25, 26, 27 (top), 30: Shutterstock; p. 7, 9, 11 (right),18 (large), 19, 24 (large), 31, 32 (top): Dreamstime; p. 32 (bottom): Courtesy of the author, Rachelle Kreisman

This series first published by:
Red Chair Press LLC   PO Box 333   South Egremont, MA 01258-0333

Printed in the United States of America

042015 1P WRZF15

Table of Contents

Words in **bold type** are defined in the glossary.

CHAPTER 1

What is a Community?

Hooray for the **community**! A community is a place where people live, work, and play. It is made up of neighborhoods. There, you will find homes and people. Who lives in one of those neighborhoods? You! That makes you part of a community.

People in a community help each other and work together. They share roads, parks, and buildings.

Can you name some buildings in a community? They include markets, schools, libraries, and hospitals. Many people work at those places. They provide goods and services. Goods are things that people can buy or borrow, such as food and books. Services are things that people do for each other. Teaching and medical care are services.

DID YOU KNOW?

Three kinds of communities are urban, suburban, and rural. Urban areas are cities. They have tall buildings and many people. Suburban areas are near cities. People often live in houses and apartments. Rural areas have fewer people and more land. Farms and villages are often found there.

CHAPTER 2

School

Where do many kids go to learn? School! Most kids start Kindergarten around age five. That is the first year of elementary school.

Teachers plan lessons for many subjects. They teach math, reading, science, and social studies. Kids usually stay in one classroom for most of the day. They may go to other teachers for art, music, library, and gym.

DID YOU KNOW?

About 50 million kids go to public schools. Some kids go to private schools. Other kids go to school at home. How many school buildings are in your community?

Middle school often starts in grade six or seven. Then kids go to high school in ninth grade. High school lasts for four years. When students graduate, they get an award called a **diploma**.

Middle and high school kids have many teachers. Each teaches a different subject. Students may start the day in a homeroom class. *Ding!* A bell often tells them when it is time to change classes.

After high school, many students go to college. They can earn an award called a **degree**. After four years, most students earn a bachelor's degree. Some students stay in school longer to earn more degrees.

Do you want to be a teacher? If so you need a college degree. You also need a degree for many other jobs.

Schools are an important part of the community. They bring people together. Many students go to after-school activities. They join clubs and play sports. Some kids take part in plays, band, or chorus. People in the community can watch the sports games. They can also attend the plays and concerts.

FUN FACT

A long time ago, kids went to one-room schoolhouses. They all had the same teacher. How long ago was that? It was the late 1800s and early 1900s. A few one- or two-room schools are still in use today, like this one in Monterey, MA.

CHAPTER 3

Library

The library is a popular place in communities. It is filled with thousands of books. A library's media center has movies, music, and sound recordings of books. People in the community can borrow the books and media for free. How can you do that? It's easy! Get a library card. It shows that you are a library member.

The library has books for people of all ages and interests.

Some people go to the library to read. Others go to do research. People also use computers there to go on the **Internet**. They may read news from home or email friends and family.

Do you have to write a report about frogs? You can visit the library and look for books about frogs. Then, find a place to sit and read the books. If you want, you can type your report on a computer.

TRY THIS!

Have you used the online catalog at your library? If not, give it a try! A librarian will help you. The catalog lets you search for books. Type a topic, title, or author you like. The computer will give you a list of books. Write down the numbers and letters (for example, E 2 027.4 H). They tell you where to find the book. The system is called the Dewey Decimal System.

What if you need help at the library? No problem! You can ask a librarian to help you find books and other materials.

The librarian also plans programs for the community. Some members take part in book clubs. They read the same books and get together to talk about them. Authors may come by to talk and sign the books they wrote. Libraries may also show movies and host parties.

Have you ever been to the children's section of a library? It is where you will find books written just for kids.

The children's section often has story time. The librarian or other guests will read picture books aloud to visitors. Many libraries also have summer reading programs. Kids can sign up, read books, and win prizes.

JUST JOKING!

Q: What is the tallest building in the community?

A: The library. It has the most stories!

Post Office

Each community has a post office. It is the building where mail is sent and received. People can drop off letters and packages there. They can also put their mail into a mailbox. Mail carriers pick up the letters and take them to the post office.

Workers unload and sort the mail. They put the mail into different machines. One separates the thin and thick letters. Another makes the letters face the same direction.

UNITED STATES POST OFFICE

A machine reads each letter's address. It may print a **bar code** on the bottom of the letter. The code is a row of lines. What does it mean? It tells another machine where the letter is being sent. That machine reads the code and sorts the mail by location. The mail is packed and ready to go.

1

From
0 lbs 4 ozs

FIRST CLASS MAIL

ZIP

DELIVERY CONFIRMATION

Electronic Rate Approved

bar code

Trucks take the mail to nearby post offices. Mail that needs to go farther is shipped by airplane. When it lands, the mail is brought to that area's main post office. Now postal workers can deliver the mail to homes and businesses in the community.

DID YOU KNOW?

Mules and llamas carry mail and packages down an 8-mile trail to the Havasupai Indians at the bottom of the Grand Canyon in Arizona!

US MAIL

CHAPTER 5

Grocery Store

Where do most people get the food they need? They go to the local grocery store. Large grocery stores are called supermarkets. Most supermarkets have a

deli counter. People often have to take a number and wait until it is called. Then they can buy sliced meats, cheeses, and salads.

Are you looking for fresh fruits and vegetables? Go to the produce section. For breads, cakes, and cookies, stop by the bakery.

People find what they need by searching the aisles in a market. Signs often show what is found in each aisle.

Many people work in the grocery store. Trucks bring food and other items to the store. Workers unload boxes and stock the shelves. Cashiers work at the register. They scan items to tell people how much money they owe. Some workers put groceries in bags for shoppers.

CHAPTER 6

Hospital

When people get sick or hurt, they may have to go to a hospital. It is open all day and night. Most hospitals are busy places with many workers. Doctors and nurses give patients medical care to help them get well.

If you go to a hospital, your parents will sign you in. You will get an ID bracelet with your name on it. First, you will see a nurse. Then a doctor will give you a checkup.

hospital ID bracelet

EMERGENCY

Drivers know to move out of the way when an ambulance is coming.

Do you need medical care right away? You can go to the hospital's emergency room. An ambulance may be called to take you there quickly. When the lights and siren are on, cars must move out of the way. Emergency medical workers take care of you on the way to the hospital.

A patient may need to stay overnight at the hospital. If that happens, the hospital is ready. Many rooms have beds for patients. They can watch TV and eat their meals in bed.

If you have to stay overnight, you will not be alone. At most hospitals, a parent can stay with you. Friends and family can visit during the day.

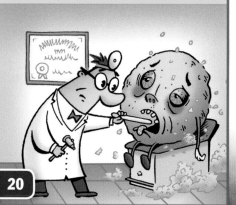

JUST JOKING!

Q: Why did the cookie go to the hospital?

A: It was feeling crumby!

The hospital also has other rooms. If you need **surgery**, you are taken to the operating room. A doctor or nurse will give you medicine so you can sleep. After the surgery is over, you wake up in the recovery room.

The hospital also has a maternity ward. That is where mothers deliver babies. Nurses and doctors take care of newborns in the nursery.

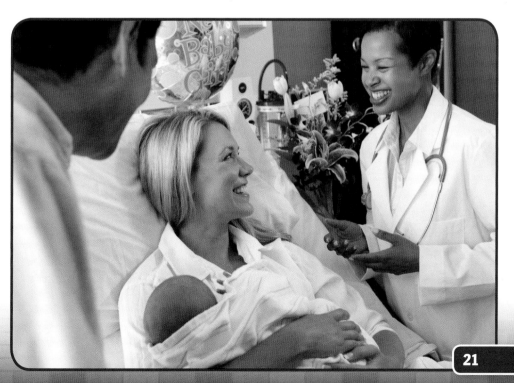

CHAPTER 7

Gas Station

Most cars and small trucks use gasoline to run. People go to gas stations to buy the fuel. At self-service stations, people can pump their own gas. At full-service stations, only **attendants** are allowed to pump the gas.

Gas stations sell different kinds of fuel. Many cars use regular gas. Others take diesel gas. Thousands of gas stations keep all the cars, trucks and farm equipment going. Small towns and rural areas may have only one station.

⌂ Gasoline for pumps is kept underground at gas stations.

The fuel comes out of a pump through a hose. People place the hose nozzle into the car's gas tank. When the nozzle handle is squeezed, the gas flows out. A meter shows the amount of gas being pumped and the price. People can let go of the handle to stop the pump.

Gasoline is kept in storage tanks underneath the ground. When the supply is low, trucks deliver more fuel to the station.

DID YOU KNOW?

Many gas stations also have air pumps. If a car tire is low on air, people can use the air pump to fill it.

CHAPTER 8

Bank

A bank is a safe place for people to keep money. A customer can go to the bank and see a bank teller. The teller will help that person put money into a bank account. The teller can also help the customer take out money.

Money kept in a savings account earns more money. That money is called **interest**. People can also go to a bank to borrow money. They have to pay the money back over time.

Banks also offer people **credit cards**. A credit card can be used to buy things. People pay the money to the bank later. If a person doesn't pay the money on time, he or she has to pay it back with interest, or more money.

A customer can also open a checking account. He or she can get **checks** or a **debit card** to pay for things. The money comes out of the checking account.

CHAPTER 9

So Many Places

People have so many places to go for goods and services. That makes life in the community much easier. Lucky you! You get to attend school and go to the library. When you are older, you can get a job. With the money you earn, you can open a bank account. You can also use the money to buy things you need, such as food and gas.

Someday, you might even want to work at one of those places! You could be a doctor and work at the hospital. You could be a teacher, a librarian, or a bank worker. Each community has so many different jobs. One may be just right for you!

TRY THIS!

Each community has places to meet people's needs. How many other places in your community can you name? (Here is a hint to get started: Where can you buy clothes? Where do people go to worship?) Do you have a favorite building in your community? Research what goods or services it provides.

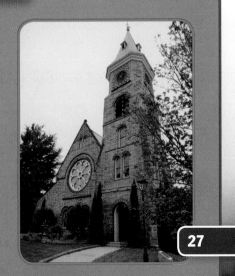

Glossary

attendant: a worker who provides a service to customers

bar code: a code of lines placed on an item so a computer can get information about the item

checks: a written order used to pay for things with money from a person's checking account

credit card: a card people can use to buy things and pay the money later

community: places where people live, work, and play

debit card: a card used to pay for things with money from a person's checking account

degree: an award a student can earn by graduating from college

diploma: an award a student can earn by graduating from high school

interest: money the bank pays to people who have a bank account; or money charged by the bank for borrowed money

Internet: a network of computers that lets people share information

rural area: an area in the country

suburban area: an area near a city

surgery: a medical operation

urban area: a city

What Did You Learn?

See how much you learned about places in a community. Answer *true* or *false* for each statement below. Write your answers on a separate piece of paper.

1 Students who go to college can earn a degree.
True or false?

2 Some mail is shipped to the post office by airplane.
True or false?

3 Cake is found in a supermarket's produce section.
True or false?

4 All gas stations let people pump their own gas.
True or false?

5 Customers can use credit cards to buy things.
True or false?

Answers: 1. True, 2. True, 3. False (Cake is found in the bakery. Fruit and vegetables are found in the produce section.), 4. False (Full-service stations have workers to pump the gas.), 5. True

For More Information

Books

Bennett, Howard J. *Harry Goes to the Hospital.* Magination Press, 2008.

Bourgeois, Paulette. *Postal Workers.* Kids Can Press, 2005.

Caseley, Judith. *On the Town: A Community Adventure.* Greenwillow Books, 2002.

Frederick, Dawn. *How It Happens at the Post Office.* Clara House Books, 2002.

Kalman, Bobbie. *What is a Community from A to Z?* Crabtree Publishing Company, 2000.

Web Sites

Ben's Guide to U.S. Government for Kids
http://bensguide.gpo.gov/k-2/neighborhood

National Postal Museum: Activity Zone
http://npm.si.edu/activity/8_activity.html

KidsHealth: Going to the Hospital
http://kidshealth.org/kid/feel_better/places/hospital.html

PBS Kids: Arthur Supermarket Adventure
http://pbskids.org/arthur/games/supermarket

Education.com: Career Information (Teacher)
http://www.education.com/reference/article/career-information-teacher/

Note to educators and parents: Our editors have carefully reviewed these web sites to ensure they are suitable for children. Web sites change frequently, however, and we cannot guarantee that a site's future contents will continue to meet our high standards of quality and educational value. You may wish to preview these sites and closely supervise children whenever they access the Internet.

Index

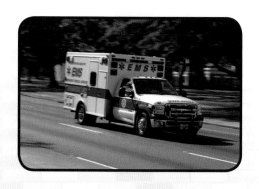

About the Author

Rachelle Kreisman has been a children's writer and editor for many years. She is the author of several children's books and hundreds of *Weekly Reader* classroom magazines. When Rachelle is not writing, she enjoys going to places in her community. She likes taking walks, hiking, biking, kayaking, and doing yoga.